Daily and Weekly Worship: Jewish and Christian

Roger T. Beckwith

Warden of Latimer House, Oxford

First published in Great Britain by
The Paternoster Press Ltd.,
Paternoster House,
3 Mount Radford Crescent,
Exeter,
Devon EX2 4JW.

This edition published by permission.

BV
185
.B4
1987

THE COVER PICTURE
is by Peter Ashton

First Grove Books Limited Edition March 1987
ISSN 0951–2667
ISBN 1 85174 048 1

GROVE BOOKS LIMITED
Bramcote   Nottingham   NG9 3DS

CONTENTS

THE ALCUIN CLUB and
GROUP FOR RENEWAL OF WORSHIP (GROW)

The Alcuin Club exists to promote the study of Christian liturgy in general and in particular the liturgies of the Anglican Communion. Since its foundation in 1897 it has published over 120 books and pamphlets. Members of the Club pay a single subscription for the year, and, from 1987 onwards, receive four Joint Liturgical Studies, and other publications of the Club, each year. Address for queries: The Alcuin Club, 5 St. Andrews Street, London EC4A 3AB.

The Group for Renewal of Worship has been responsible since 1971 for the Grove Booklets on Ministry and Worship (now the Grove Worship Series), and since 1975 for the quarterly scholarly 'Grove Liturgical Studies'. This latter series has been phased into the new Studies. The address is that of Grove Books Limited, publishers of these Studies.

The Joint Liturgical Studies, beginning from March 1987, represent the coming together of the concerns and resources of both earlier groups, and they are planned and edited by a Joint Editorial Board appointed from both groups. The new Studies are published quarterly by Grove Books Limited. At the time of publishing the Joint Editorial Board consists of the following:

Colin Buchanan (Chairman of GROW)
Geoffrey Cuming
John Fenwick
Donald Gray (Chairman of the Alcuin Club)
Trevor Lloyd
Michael Vasey

The titles for 1987 and previous titles are listed at the back of this book. Their retail price in 1987 is £2.50 each.

The substance of this three-part essay was first delivered as a pair of lectures at the Liturgical Institute of the Catholic University of Louvain on 24 April 1980. Its author is warden of Latimer House, an Anglican theological research centre at Oxford, and has written on the Jewish and early Christian liturgy in the journals Revue de Qumran, Studia Liturgica *etc. and in the volumes* This is the Day: the Biblical Doctrine of the Christian Sunday in its Jewish and Early Church Setting *(with W. Stott, London, Marshall, Morgan & Scott, 1978) and* The Study of Liturgy *(ed. Jones, Wainwright & Yarnold, London, S.P.C.K., 1978). An uncorrected text of this article appeared in* Questions Liturgiques *62:1 (1981), and it is here reprinted by permission from the corrected text published in* The Evangelical Quarterly *56:2, 3 (1984), with a few small changes.*

I. INTRODUCTION

The words of Jesus in the Sermon on the Mount 'Think not that I came to destroy the Law or the Prophets: I came not to destroy but to fulfil' (Mt. 5:17), apply as much to worship as they do to other aspects of the Christian gospel. The originality of Christian worship is not that it abolishes Jewish worship but that it reforms and develops that worship, in accordance with Jesus' teaching and in recognition of his saving work. Thus, the background to Christian worship is, at the outset, Judaism, and especially Jewish worship, as established in the Old Testament and as practised in the first century. By studying this we learn to recognise what is new in Christian worship, as well as what is old.

Study of the Jewish background of Christian worship is, however, complicated by many factors:

(i). The period of direct contact and influence was comparatively short, being largely confined to the first century AD, by the end of which the breach between Church and Synagogue was probably almost complete.[1] Later evidence about Jewish and Christian worship must, there-

---

[1] According to a baraita or ancient quotation in the Babylonian Talmud (Berakoth 28b-29a), it was around the end of the first century that the *birkath ha-minim* (benediction about the heretics) in the Jewish liturgy was composed by Samuel the Less. In its old Palestinian form, this is bitterly anti-Christian: see C. W. Dugmore, *The Influence of the Synagogue upon the Divine Office* (London, Faith Press edition, 1964), 3f., 119f. Note also Rev. 2:9; 3:9. The strongest link between Jews and Christians would have been the Jewish Christians of Palestine, and as these conformed increasingly to Gentile Christianity, the link would have become more and more tenuous. In 135 AD, when the Jews were expelled from Jerusalem, even the church there became a Gentile body (cp. Eusebius, *Ecclesiastical History* 4:5:1-4). The Nazareans and Ebionites, who alone persisted in the literal observance of the Law, became separated from other Christians.

fore, for our purpose, be treated with caution; but the later evidence is much more abundant than the earlier.

(ii). First-century Judaism was divided into three main schools of thought, the Pharisees, the Sadducees, and the Essenes. We have much more ample evidence about Pharisaic worship than about that of the other two schools (though our knowledge of Essene worship has been markedly increased by the Dead Sea Scrolls, especially the Qumran *Book of Hymns*), nor do we know for certain which of the schools most influenced the Church.

(iii). Even within themselves, the three schools were divided by geography and language. Most of our Jewish evidence concerns Palestinian, Semitic worship. We do not really know how much like it the Hellenistic worship of the Dispersion was. Christianity, however, drew most of its early converts from Hellenistic countries outside Palestine; and though the Semitic Christianity of Syria doubtless began early, there is little surviving evidence about it from before the fourth century. This again makes comparison difficult.

(iv). Even before the end of the first century, Jewish worship was radically disturbed by the destruction of the Temple in AD 70. All Jewish and Jewish Christian evidence from after AD 70 is likely to be affected by this event.

(v). The earliest liturgical texts, both Jewish and Christian, tended to be much more fluid than later ones.[2] Though written liturgical prayers are to be found in the Old Testament,[3] the Pharisees evidently distinguished traditional prayer from biblical, with the result that the structure of their services and the themes of their prayers were apt to be fixed well

---

[2] Thus, in the Mishnah, Rabbi Joshua and Rabbi Akiba permit the substance of the 18 Benedictions to be used instead of the full text, and Rabbi Eliezer emphasises that devotion is more important than simply reciting a form (*Berakoth* 4:3f.). For such reasons, the writing down of prayers was discouraged among the Jews much longer than the writing down of legal traditions, and a baraita in the Babylonian Talmud (*Shabbath* 115b) says that 'those who write down benedictions are as though they burnt the Lawbook'. Among Christians, who shared with the Essenes a greater readiness to put prayers in writing, this situation did not continue so long, but in the earliest period the Lord's Prayer is recorded in the gospels in two different forms; *Didache* 10 permits prophets to offer thanks at the eucharist 'as much as they desire'; Justin Martyr speaks of the bishop giving thanks there 'at considerable length' or 'according to his ability' (*First Apology* 65, 67); and Hippolytus directs that 'it is not at all necessary for him (the bishop) to utter the same words as we said above, as though reciting them from memory . . . only, he must pray what is sound and orthodox' (*Apostolic Tradition* 9).

[3] Num. 5:19-22; 6:23-27; Dt. 21:6-8; 26:3-10, 13-15, and the Psalter, for the liturgical use of which see 1 Chr. 16:7-42, the Psalm titles (especially in the Septuagint of Pss. 24, 29, 38, 48, 92, 93, 94, 96), and Mishnah Bikkurim 3:4, Pesahim 5:7, Tamid 7:4. In all these passages, Tabernacle or Temple worship, not synagogue worship, is primarily in view.

before the wording was; and though there may have been *standard* forms of words, both among Pharisees and among Christians, they can seldom be recovered with certainty. This makes influence more difficult to detect.

The above considerations apply to the Jewish antecedents of all Christian worship — of initiation and ordination, for example, and not simply of daily and weekly worship. If these considerations could not reasonably be qualified, the obstacles in the way of our enquiry would be formidable indeed. Fortunately, however, each of the five can be qualified, and probably ought to be.

Regarding point (i), if the first-century evidence about Jewish and Christian worship is not abundant, it is none the less considerable, being provided by the New Testament, the writings of Philo and Josephus, and the *Didache*. In respect of Jewish worship, a good deal can also be inferred from the Old Testament and the intertestamental writings, as well as from the earliest parts of the rabbinical literature. Since the rabbinical literature is a written record of Pharisaic oral tradition, it is likely to contain a lot of older material, and the Mishnah, written at the turn of the second and third centuries AD, may well comprise many first century traditions, and also show the outworking in the second century of tendencies established in the first.[4] The same is true of the Tosephta, the Halakic Midrashim, the baraitas (sayings quoted from old rabbinical compilations other than the Mishnah) included in the two Talmuds, and Targum Neofiti, which are likewise of relatively early date, probably third-century. The light which these writings throw on Jewish worship is most important, as Jewish Prayer Books begin to appear only in the ninth century.

Regarding point (ii), the statements of Josephus and the rabbis that Pharisaism was the *prevailing* school of thought in the first century (and indeed earlier), so much so that even the Sadducean chief priests had normally to fall in with Pharisaic views in practice, are probably reliable.[5] Pharisaic worship, therefore, is what we mainly need to know

---

4 An example of a parallel (but not identical) development in Jewish and Christian worship of the second century, which presumably went back to a common tendency in the first, is the centralisation of rabbinical ordination in the national patriarch and of Christian ordination in the diocesan bishop. Other examples will be seen below, namely, the development of daily prayers into corporate services, and the use of Psalms 145-150, at first by individuals, but later by congregations.

5 Josephus, who was no bigoted Pharisee, repeatedly states this (*Antiquities* 13:288, 296, 298, 401f.; 18:15, 17), and the rabbinical literature lends him independent support. The extraordinary prominence of the Pharisees in the gospels is suggestive of the same thing. In the synagogues, the Sadducees seem to have been completely powerless.

about, though Essenism seems also to have influenced the Church to some extent.

Regarding point (iii), we know that Hellenistic Judaism looked to Palestine as its mother country, constantly made festal pilgrimages to Jerusalem, translated much Palestinian literature, and imitated Palestinian institutions to a high degree. Moreover, the penetration of Greek language and culture into Palestine was greater than used to be supposed, so there was influence from both sides, and the barrier between the two forms of Judaism cannot have been enormous. As to worship, we know that the Scriptures were read and expounded in the Hellenistic synagogues, as in the Semitic,[6] and that the Hellenistic synagogues were likewise places of prayer;[7] and, as to the forms of prayer that were used, the regulation in the Mishnah that the Shema and the Tephillah, the two chief synagogue prayers, may be said in any language (Sotah 7:1), is no doubt significant. Consequently, it is not a hopeless quest to look for signs of the influence of Jewish worship in the Greek and Latin Christianity of the second and third centuries, or, with regard to a country like Syria, where the Semitic language and culture made Jewish influence more obvious and more persistent, in the Christianity of the fourth and even later centuries.[8]

Regarding point (iv), the effects of the destruction of the Temple, though profound, are relatively easy to identify. For the Jews, the destruction made synagogue worship a *substitute* for Temple worship, instead of being a *complement* to it, which is what it had previously been, except among the Jews of the Dispersion and the excommunicated Essenes. Also, the destruction doubtless accentuated the tendency, which may already have been present in Jewish liturgical texts, to spiritualise the idea of sacrifice. Furthermore, it brought the festal pilgrimages to an end, and so made the Passover meal a more purely domestic occasion, observed at home and not in a borrowed room at Jerusalem, and regularly involving the whole family. For Jewish Christians, the destruction must have dealt a severe blow to their practice of maintaining Jewish ordinances alongside the Christian counterparts of those ordinances—circumcision alongside baptism (Acts 2:38-41; 21:20f. etc), the Passover meal alongside the

---

6 Acts 13:15, 27; 15:21; Philo, *Hypothetica* 7:12f.; *Quod Omnis Probus Liber Sit* 81f.
7 Philo's usual name for the synagogue is *proseuche*, 'place of prayer' (*In Flaccum* 41, 45 etc.; *De Legatione ad Gaium* 132, 138 etc.), a name which is applied to the synagogue in Egyptian inscriptions and papyri from the third century BC onwards.
8 In Syrian Christianity, one has also to allow for the possibility that some of the Jewish influence may be of later date than the first century, and that there may be reciprocal influence, Christianity upon Judaism as well as Judaism upon Christianity.

eucharist,[9] and the sabbath day alongside Sunday.[10] After the destruction, the majority of Jewish Christians, being estranged by now from the non-Christian Jews, probably conformed increasingly to Gentile Christianity;[11] a second group seem to have tried, as far as was practicable, to maintain the *status quo* (these became the Nazareans, and the more orthodox Ebionites — if the two are not, in fact, the same); while a third group, who became the more heretical Ebionites, apparently reacted away from the Church, in some matters towards non-Christian Judaism (abandoning Sunday observance, and retaining the eucharist only at Passover time), in some matters towards Encratism (using water for the eucharistic cup) and in some matters (notably Christological) towards Gnosticism.

Regarding point (v), what this means is that apparent echoes of *wording* from Jewish prayers to Christian must be treated with caution: the variety of forms in which, for example, the Tephillah exists, make it doubtful whether even a *standard* form of words was memorised. At the same time, the *structure* and *themes* of the traditional Jewish prayers (just like the *constituents* of the traditional Jewish services) show remarkable stability, and the references to them in the earliest rabbinical literature, from before the time when they were written down, are perfectly recognisable. Much the same is, of course, true of early Christian services and prayers, which started being written down considerably sooner. Even the caution about wording must be qualified in one respect, which is that some formulas and linguistic conventions are so regular in Jewish prayers that they had probably been habitual from very early times, and can therefore be compared with the corresponding formulas and linguistic conventions in Christian prayers.

---

9   Since the Jewish Christians for many years went on offering sacrifices in the Temple (Acts 21:23-26), there is every reason to suppose that, for as long as they did, they went on offering the Passover lamb and observing the Passover meal.

10 The more orthodox group of the Ebionites observed both, Eusebius tells us (*Ecclesiastical History* 3:27-5), and that is just what we would expect of their Jewish-Christian predecessors. A. F. J. Klijn and G. J. Reinink dismiss Eusebius's statement (*Patristic Evidence for Jewish-Christian Sects,* Supplements to Novum Testamentum 36, Leiden, Brill, 1973, 25-28), but this seems rash. Eusebius's great learning, and the general consistency of his account of the Ebionites with other patristic accounts, entitle it to more respect.

11 Whether they continued to observe the sabbath, as is sometimes supposed, must be reckoned very doubtful. The liturgical observance of the sabbath which is found in fourth-century texts from Syria and elsewhere could either be a survival or a restoration: Wilfrid Stott argues cogently that it the latter (*This is the Day, ut supra,* 51). Possibly the residual respect for the sabbath which had led Tertullian (*On Fasting* 14f.) and Hippolytus (*Commentary on Daniel* 4:20) to oppose fasting on that day, and had led others mentioned by Tertullian to refrain from kneeling on that day (*On Prayer* 23), was the basis on which the fourth-century liturgical observance of the day was erected.

II. THE CENTRES, PATTERNS AND ELEMENTS OF JEWISH WORSHIP

Jewish worship of the first century, up to 70 AD, had three centres, the Temple, the synagogue and the home. Temple worship, based on the regulations of the Mosaic Law, was daily, and was primarily sacrificial, with additional sacrifices on sabbaths, new moons and annual holy days. Liturgical texts from the Old Testament were used with some of the sacrifices, however;[12] psalms were sung, different ones being appointed for the different days of the week, for the presentation of firstfruits and for festivals;[13] Scripture was publicly read on the Day of Atonement and at Tabernacles;[14] the rabbis taught at festivals;[15] and traditional prayers were used, which often corresponded in general to the Shema and Tephillah of the synagogue, but had certain unique features. Thus, every morning, in the course of the morning sacrifice, the priests said the Shema almost in full and a much abbreviated Tephillah (Mishnah Tamid 5:1); and after the Scripture-reading on the Day of Atonement and at Tabernacles eight benedictions were said, three of which corresponded to benedictions of the Tephillah (Mishnah Yoma 7:1, Sotah 7.7f.).[16] Attention is drawn by the Mishnah to various verbal and formal peculiarities of the Temple prayers over against those of the synagogue, even where they otherwise corresponded closely, which show that Temple-prayer, though intimately related to that of the synagogue, had a significant measure of independence.[17] This is not surprising when one remembers that the most ancient Jewish prayers (those prescribed in the Old Testament) were first used in the Tabernacle or Temple,[18] that the

12 See note 3.
13 See note 3.
14 See Mishnah Yoma 7:1, Sotah 7:7f., and cp. Deut. 31:10-13.
15 See Lk. 2:46f., and cp. the practice of Jesus in Mat. 21:23; Mk. 14:49; Jn. 7:14, 28; 8:20, 18:20.
16 Joseph Heinemann has plausibly suggested that these eight benedictions were one of the earlier series out of which the eighteen of the Tephillah had been compiled, and that another such series was the seven which are substituted for the eighteen in the synagogue on sabbaths and festivals (*Prayer in the Talmud: Forms and Patterns*, Studia Judaica 9, Berlin, De Gruyter, 1977, 218-221, 226-29). One would not expect a *shorter* series (the first three and last three of the eighteen, with a special one in between) to be substituted on sabbaths and festivals, and the theory that this is an older tradition would explain the anomaly.
17 Thus, the divine name was used without paraphrase in Temple prayers, they regularly ended 'for ever and ever' or 'from everlasting to everlasting', the response to them was 'Blessed be the name of the glory of his kingdom for ever and ever', and the Aaronic blessing was not broken up with Amens (Mishnah Berakoth 9:5, Yoma 3:8; 4:2; 6:2, Sotah 7:6, Tamid 7:2).
18 Namely, the prayers listed in note 3, together with the high priest's confession on the Day of Atonement (Lev. 16:21), the traditional text of which is given by the Mishnah (Yoma 6:2).

public reading of Scripture originated in and around it (Deut. 31:10f; 2 Kings 23:2; Neh. 8:1-18), and that the duty of teaching the Law was originally imposed upon the priests and Levites (Lev. 10:11; Deut. 17:11; 24:8; 33:10; Hos. 4:6; Hg. 2:11; Mal. 2:5-7 etc.): so that all the elements of synagogue worship – prayer, Scripture reading and teaching – had a Temple background. Consequently, though they were developed more highly in the synagogue than in the Temple, partly because the priesthood had other duties and partly because it culpably neglected teaching, the hypothesis that the synagogue arose because the Temple was distant or in ruin or simply in decline, and not independently, is much the most probable.[19]

Though the synagogue developed the ministry of the word and prayer more highly than the Temple, for which reason synagogues were found even in Jerusalem, it had its chief usefulness away from Jerusalem, where it enabled Jews to fulfil duties and enjoy privileges which would otherwise have been completely impossible. It enabled Jews who could not get to the Temple still to observe the 'holy convocations' of Lev. 23, that is, to assemble for worship on the days there listed, which are the weekly sabbath and the annual holy days. There was no need for synagogue services on ordinary weekdays, which were not among the prescribed 'holy convocations', and even in the New Testament period such services were exceptional. Only in the Temple, where the daily sacrifices were offered, did the people of the locality pray together daily. The Mishnah tells us that in the synagogues of some towns there were services on Mondays and Thursdays, these being days when law courts assembled there (Megillah 1:3; 3:6-4:1); and that for two weeks in the year the lay *maamad*, or embryo congregation, corresponding to a particular priestly course, held daily services in a synagogue (Taanith 4:1-5 etc); but that is all. For the rest, the constant references to sabbath-day services, and to no others, that we find in first-century literature, speak for themselves.[20] Of course, the synagogues in some places may have been open on weekdays for individuals who wanted to use them, but this is quite another matter than holding regular, organized services of a corporate kind there. It seems,

---

[19] For a recent discussion of the origin of the synagogue, see H. H. Rowley, *Worship in Ancient Israel* (London, S.P.C.K., 1967), 213-229.

[20] See Lk. 4:16-27; Acts 13:14-43; 15:21; Philo, *De Vita Mosis* 2:216; *De Specialibus Legibus* 2:62f.; *Quod Omnis Probus Liber Sit* 80-82; *De Vita Contemplativa* 30-33; *Hypothetica* 7:12f.; *De Legatione ad Gaium* 156f; Josephus, *Antiquities* 16:43, 164; *Against Apion* 1:209; 2:175. Only in Philo's account of the Essenes do we read that instruction is given 'at all other times' as well as on the sabbath (*Quod Omnis Probus* 81), and this is explained by the Essenes' communal life. For further discussion, see *This is the Day, ut supra,* 151, and the literature there cited.

consequently, to be a serious misconception on the part of Joseph Heinemann to take Jesus's rebuke to the Pharisees for 'loving to stand and pray
in the synagogues and in the corners of the streets, that they may be seen
of men' (Matt. 6:5) as an attack on the synagogue services.[21] It probably
has nothing to do with the sabbath-day services, in which Jesus, as Luke
tells us, regularly took part (Lk. 4:16), but applies rather to the prayers of
the individual on weekdays. The reference to 'the corners of the streets'
sufficiently indicates this. Jesus is not rebuking corporate prayers but
individual prayers prayed in public, for purposes of ostentation. It is true,
as Heinemann says, that when Jesus drew up a model prayer for his
disciples, he drew up a much shorter and simpler one than the Tephillah,
probably in Aramaic rather than in Hebrew, and akin in character to
Jewish private prayers of a non-statutory kind,[22] but this is a very different
thing from opposing corporate prayer in principle. The Lord's Prayer
itself, though taught in Matthew in the context of private prayer (Matt.
6:5-15), has proved quite adaptable for corporate use also, and, in view of
its constant employment of the first person plural, was probably intended
to be adapted for this purpose. Moreover, like the Tephillah for the Jews,
it is for Christians their statutory prayer.

The sabbath-day services of the synagogue were four in number,
Morning Prayer, Additional Prayer, Afternoon Prayer and Evening
Prayer, at each of which the Tephillah was used (Mishnah Berakoth 4:1).
Three of the services corresponded to the three hours of *daily* prayer by
individuals, which were based on Ps. 55:17 and Dan. 6:10, 13 (and so
upon the daily course of the sun), and two of which seem also to have been
linked, at an early stage, with the two hours of daily sacrifice in the
Temple; while the fourth service was linked with the additional sacrifice
of the sabbath, and was known by the same name (*musaph*, addition).
The connection of prayer with the evening sacrifice is made clear in the
Old Testament (Ezra 9:5ff.; Dan. 9:20f.): already, it seems, prayer was

---

21 *Prayer in the Talmud*, 191f.; 'The Background of Jesus' Prayer in the Jewish Liturgical
Tradition', in *The Lord's Prayer and Jewish Liturgy*, ed. J. J. Petuchowski and
M. Brocke (London, Burns & Oates, 1978).

22 *loc cit*. By contrast, the Shema and Tephillah, though they could be used individually as
well as corporately, were *statutory* prayers — the prescribed means for fulfilling the
obligation of thanksgiving and petition. Heinemann concedes that the Lord's Prayer
has similarities to the Kaddish, which is not a private prayer, but since its antiquity is not
entirely certain, this cannot be stressed. It does not really affect the contrast with the
Tephillah to point out, as G. J. Bahr does, that Jewish and Christian prayer-texts were
fluid, and that the Lord's Prayer could be and was paraphrased at much greater length
('The Use of the Lord's Prayer in the Primitive Church', in *Journal of Biblical
Literature*, 84, 1965, 153-59). The fact remains that the basic texts of the Tephillah are
immensely longer and more complicated than those of the Lord's Prayer, which could
be comprised within a single one of the eighteen benedictions of the other.

not only directed towards the Temple (1 Kings 8:29, 35, 38, 42, 44, 48; Dan. 6:10), as the place prayer would be heard, but especially at the hours when sacrifice was due to be offered there for God to accept. In the intertestamental literature and the New Testament, we read of prayer being made at the time of the offering of incense (Judith 9:1ff.; Lk. 1:10) — the evening incense in the former case, though the incense was offered both morning and evening, at the same hours — in the morning and 'between the two evenings' — as the morning and evening sacrifice (Ex. 29:39, 41; 30:7f.; Num. 28:4, 8). In the first century, the incense was offered in the actual course of the ritual of each of the daily sacrifices (Mishnah Yoma 3:5). Since Evening Prayer was so closely related to the evening sacrifice, and Additional Prayer to the additional sacrifice, there is every reason to think that Morning Prayer was similarly related to the morning sacrifice, which was apparently offered at the fourth hour of the day, or 10.00 hrs. (Mishnah Eduyoth 6:1). This relationship, however, made the old noonday hour of prayer (Ps. 55:17) look anomalous, since no sacrifice was offered at that hour, and by the first century it seems to have completely lapsed (assuming that Peter's prayer at noon in Acts 10:9 is a coincidence). What is more, the evening sacrifice, which had originally been offered at sunset,[23] had by this period been moved forward to the mid-afternoon, about the ninth hour of day, or 15.00 hrs. (Josephus, *Antiquities* 14:65; Mishnah Pesahim 5:1). Practical reasons have been suggested for this change, but it may rather have been due to an interpretation of 'between the two evenings' similar to that of the Essenes, who took it to mean from 14.00 hrs. onwards (Jubilees 49:1, 10-12). The hour of prayer had moved with the offering, as we can see from Acts 3:1; 10:3, 30, and hence the institution of Afternoon Prayer. This move, however, had tended to make *Evening* Prayer anomalous, like the old hour of prayer at noon, and the Mishnah consequently concedes that the evening Tephillah has no fixed hour (Berakoth 4:1), while the Babylonian Talmud reports a dispute between Rabban Gamaliel II and Rabbi Joshua around the end of the first century, in which Rabbi Joshua maintains that the evening Tephillah is optional (Berakoth 27b). What probably saved Evening Prayer was that at morning and evening the Shema was said as well as the Tephillah (Mishnah Berakoth 1:1f.). The Shema could not so easily be moved to a different time of day, since it incorporates Deut. 6:4-9, which is to be said 'when you lie down and when you rise up', and includes benedictions which differ from evening to morning and refer to the time of day.

---

[23] This is how 'between the two evenings' is glossed by Deut. 16:6 (for the phrase is used elsewhere of the Passover offering), and the fact that 'between the two evenings' was the hour of the lighting of the lamps in the Tabernacle (Ex. 30:8) implies the same thing.

The Essenes, however, seem to have resolved the problem in their own way by reducing the daily hours of prayer from three to two, at sunrise and at sunset. This is clearly stated of the closely related Therapeutae by Philo (*De Vita Contemplativa* 27), and, in the Qumran literature, is the most probable meaning of *Manual of Discipline* 9:26-10:3; 10:10, and *Book of Hymns* 12:4-9. Whether, like the Pharisees, the Essenes had an extra hour of prayer on the sabbath, making the total three on that occasion, we do not know for certain: but the work *Songs of the Sabbath Sacrifice* found at Qumran, and the blowing of trumpets, for the sabbath assemblies, presumably at the hours of sacrifice (*Damascus Document* 11:22f.; cp. Num. 10:2f. 10), make this likely.

The standard pattern of first-century Jewish worship was therefore as follows: the use of the Shema twice each day, in the morning and evening, and the use of the Tephillah three times each day, in the morning, afternoon and evening, with an additional Tephillah — which might be at any hour — on the sabbath (Mishnah Berakoth 1:1f.; 4:1). When the use of the Shema and Tephillah in the morning or evening was combined, as in corporate use it naturally was, this resulted in three daily hours of prayer, with a fourth on the sabbath. The Essenes probably reduced the number by one, using their own prayers instead of the Shema and Tephillah. However, if at the beginning of the Christian era the evening Shema and Tephillah were said privately, even on the sabbath (which is what some scholars infer from the dispute about Evening Prayer),[24] it means that the corporate services of the sabbath, in both traditions, numbered three.

Thanksgiving and Prayer (the Shema and Tephillah)
The Shema is earlier attested than the Tephillah, the oldest evidence for the former being the allusion in the Letter of Aristeas (Ep. Ar. 158-160) or perhaps even earlier the fragment in the Nash papyrus, which dates from about 150 BC. In this fragment the Ten Commandments are followed by the introduction to Deut. 6:4-9, the first of the readings in the traditional Shema (hence its name, which means 'Hear!'), the remaining two readings being Deut. 11:13-21 and Num. 15:37-41. These three passages are intended as a summary of the Law, and contain the Great Commandment, together with the rules about phylacteries on arm and head, mezuzoth on doorways and fringes on garments — the various visible reminders of the Law in daily life. Originally, however, as we know from Mishnah Tamid 5:1, these three passages were preceded by the Decalogue; and the two Talmuds tell us that it was only omitted because

---

[24] See Ismar Elbogen, *Der jüdische Gottesdienst in seiner geschichtlichen Entwicklung* (Hildesheim, Olms reprint, 1962), 99f.

of 'the insinuations of the heretics', namely, that the Ten Commandments were the sole part of the Law that was revealed to Moses on Sinai (Jerusalem Berakoth 1:4; Babylonian Berakoth 12a). At the Palestinian synagogue of Old Cairo, however, the Decalogue continued to be included at least until the year 1211.[25] The 'heretics' in question are most likely the early Christians,[26] who did sometimes make a sharp distinction between the Decalogue, as the original and permanent part of the Law, and the ceremonial precepts, added only after the sin of the golden calf (Irenaeus, *Against Heresies* 4:15:1f.; *Didascalia* 2, 26). Before the four (now three) passages from the Law come two benedictions, the first a thanksgiving for creation (adapted to the morning or evening hour, as the case may be) and the second a thanksgiving for revelation; the latter forms a natural introduction to the passages from the Law. After these passages, with equal appropriateness, comes a benediction in thanksgiving for Israel's redemption from Egypt, and finally, in the evening only, one is added as a prayer for rest.[27] The benedictions are mentioned in the Mishnah, by number and in some cases by name (Berakoth 1:4; 2:2; Tamid 5:1), and they are noticed in general terms by Josephus, who makes this remarkable allusion to the Shema, referring to the hours at which it is said, the passages from the Law and the benedictions (especially the third of them):

'Twice every day, at the dawn thereof, and when the hour comes for turning to repose, let all acknowledge before God the bounties which he has bestowed on them through their deliverance from the land of Egypt: thanksgiving is a natural duty, and is rendered alike in gratitude for past mercies and to incline the giver to others yet to come. They shall inscribe also on their doors the greatest of the benefits which they have received from God and each shall display them on his arms; and all that can show forth the power of God and his goodwill towards them, let them bear a record thereof written on the head and on the arm, so that men may see on every side the loving care with which God surrounds them' (*Antiquities* 14:212f., Thackeray's translation).

---

25 See Jacob Mann in J. J. Petuchowski, ed. *Contributions to the Scientific Study of Jewish Liturgy* (New York, Ktav, 1970), 393f.

26 For the view that these heretics are not Christians but Hellenistic Jews, see Geza Vermes, *Post-Biblical Jewish Studies* (Studies in Judaism in Late Antiquity 8, Leiden, Brill, 1975), 169-177.

27 English translations of these benedictions (according to the Northern French and German use) may be found in Simeon Singer, *The Authorised Daily Prayer Book*, first published in 1891 and often reprinted. Translations of two versions of the Tephillah may be found in C. W. Dugmore, *The Influence of the Synagogue upon the Divine Office, ut supra*, 114-125. German translations are given by Strack-Billerbeck in their *Kommentar zum Neuen Testament aus Talmud und Midrasch* (Munich, Beck, 1954-56 reprint), excursus 9 and 10, 'Das Shema' and 'Das Shemone-Esre'.

The Centres, Patterns and Elements of Jewish Worship 15

It is noteworthy that Josephus puts these words into the mouth of Moses, and includes them in a paraphrase of the book of Deuteronomy, which shows that he thinks the use of the Shema to be implied in the Old Testament itself and to be of extreme antiquity. Equally noteworthy is the fact that he conceives the Shema as, above all, a thanksgiving for deliverance from the land of Egypt. Sometimes the Shema is viewed as a confession of faith, because it includes the statement of the unity of God in Deut. 6:4; sometimes, following the Mishnah, it is viewed as an act of self-dedication, of 'taking upon oneself the yoke of the kingdom of heaven', because it contains the Great Commandment (Berakoth 2:2); but the most ancient characterization of it is that of Josephus, who interprets it, in accordance with its third and culminating benediction, as an act of thanksgiving for redemption.

The Tephillah, or Amidah, or Eighteen Benedictions, is not so early attested, though it was well established by the time of the Mishnah, which states that its benedictions are eighteen in number (Berakoth 4:3; Taanith 2:2) and names individually the first three, the last three, and three others (Berakoth 5:2; Yoma 7:1; Rosh ha-Shanah 4:5; Sotah 7:7; Tamid 5:1). The earliest rabbis whom the Mishnah mentions as discussing it lived at about 100 AD, when Rabban Gamaliel II ruled that it was to be said daily (Berakoth 4:3f., 7), and a baraita in the Babylonian Talmud records that it was drawn up according to its present arrangement at about that date (Berakoth 28b-29a). We have already noted Heinemann's plausible suggestion that it was compiled from earlier series of benedictions (see note 16), and it would be rash to assume that prior to this time the three traditional hours of daily prayer were observed in a completely different manner. However, it is clear from the New Testament that it was still possible in the earlier part of the first century for individual teachers — and especially for teachers with prophetic claims, like John the Baptist and Jesus — to draw up their own tephillah for their disciples to use (Lk. 11:1-4).

The word 'tephillah' simply means 'prayer' (the alternative title 'amidah' referring to the 'standing' position in which it was said), and, if the Shema is the great thanksgiving of the ancient Jewish liturgy, the Tephillah is its great petitionary prayer. Today it consists of nineteen benedictions, not eighteen, apparently because in Babylonia, where the Jewish liturgy was given its final form, the fourteenth benediction was divided into two.[28] It is striking that a petition should take the form of

28 See Heinemann, *Prayer in the Talmud, ut supra,* 22, 67, 224-26. A comparison with the Palestinian form, printed from a Cairo Genizah MS. by Solomon Schechter, makes this likely: for the Palestinian text, see Petuchowski, *Contributions to the Scientific Study of Jewish Liturgy, ut supra,* 377f., and for a translation, C. W. Dugmore, as cited in note

benedictions—of blessing the Lord. The first three and penultimate benedictions do, in fact, consist of praise and thanksgiving, and not of petition, but the remaining benedictions are petitionary, and only justify their title because they close with a sentence blessing God that he does in fact give the particular benefit (forgiveness, the fruits of the earth, the restoration of Israel, or whatever it may be) for which the benediction has asked. One cannot avoid the conclusion that the Tephillah is an example of a pious but highly stylised mode of prayer.

Interpolated into the Tephillah are certain important passages of Scripture. Before the last benediction, the theme of which is peace, comes the Aaronic blessing from Num. 6:22-27, as the Mishnah mentions (Rosh ha-Shanah 4:5; Megillah 4:3, 5; Tamid 5:1). Also, as a congregational response to the third benediction, the theme of which is God's holiness, the Kedushah is used. This is a series of verses beginning with Is. 6:3, first mentioned in Tosephta Berakoth 1:9, and also used with the first morning benediction of the Shema, the theme of which is the glory due to God for his creation.

Apart from the benedictions said by individuals on weekdays and by congregations on the sabbath, there were also the benedictions said in families and among friends at meals and similar domestic occasions. Graces at meals were practised both by the Essenes and by the Pharisees. Josephus speaks of grace being said for the gift of life both before and after Essene common meals (*War* 2:131); the Qumran literature speaks of grace before meals (*Manual of Discipline* 6:3-8; *Messianic Rule*, 1 Q Sa. 2:17f.); while the book of Jubilees gives an example of a grace in which God is blessed for his creation after a meal (Jub. 22:6). The Letter of Aristeas quotes a petitionary grace before a meal for the continual enjoyment of God's gifts (Ep. Ar. 183-85); but in all the forms given in the Mishnah (Berakoth, chs. 6 and 7) God is blessed, and not just for the meal in general but for particular foodstuffs, for bread and for wine, each in a separate benediction, so that the meal would be punctuated by a number of graces, as at the miraculous feedings in the gospels, and the Last Supper. If three or more men were present, the meal concluded with a more elaborate grace over 'the cup of the blessing', called the 'Common Grace' or the 'Three Benedictions'. These three benedictions, as we know from other rabbinical sources, blessed God for the food, thanked him for the land and prayed for his mercy upon the people of Israel and the city of

---

27. The new benediction against heretics (see note 1), which has sometimes been supposed to explain the Babylonian number, occurs in both versions as benediction 12, and may have been an adaptation of an earlier benediction rather than an addition to the prayer.

Jerusalem.[29] The opening biddings to the Common Grace in the Mishnah envisage that very large numbers may sometimes be present, and Heinemann supposes these forms to have originated in the meals of the Pharisaic haburoth — groups of Pharisaic 'associates', who were willing to eat together from time to time because they had all undertaken to tithe their foodstuffs scrupulously and to observe strictly the rules of ceremonial cleanness.[30] A similar procedure would, however, be followed at any formal meal,[31] and this included (allowing for certain peculiarities) the Passover meal, which in the first century was held by the pilgrims in a borrowed room of a Jerusalem house, their numbers having grown too great to be accommodated any longer by the Temple courts. A passover-company consisted of those who could consume one lamb, which might mean one or more families, or else a group of men like Jesus and his disciples, since it was, strictly speaking, only incumbent upon males to go up to Jerusalem for the Passover (Ex. 23:17; 34:23; Deut. 16:16). Back at home, the chief meal of the week was the evening meal at the beginning of the sabbath, the evening meal being the chief meal of the day (the other being breakfast, between about 10.00 and 12.00 hrs.)[32] and the sabbath being the festive day. At this meal, already in the first century, a benediction was said over a cup of wine, both for the wine and for the day, as the discussions between the first-century Pharisaic schools of Shammai and Hillel show (Mishnah Berakoth 8:1-4), and another important event at about the same hour was the lighting of the sabbath lamp (Mishnah Shabbath 2:6f.), the kindling of fire being prohibited after the sabbath had begun. A blessing for light was said at the close of the sabbath the following evening, when the restriction on kindling ended and the day of the creation of light, Sunday, began. This benediction also was already in existence in the first century, when it was discussed by Beth Shammai and Beth Hillel (Mishnah Berakoth 8:5f.).

The Ministry of the Word
In all this, we have said nothing about the reading of the Scriptures and teaching, which existed both in the home from day to day and in the synagogue on the sabbath, and are the features of sabbath-day worship

---

[29] See Joachim Jeremias, *The Eucharistic Words of Jesus* (English translation, London, S.C.M., 1966), 110, following Finkelstein. A fourth benediction was later added.
[30] 'Birkath ha-Zimmun and Havurah-Meals', in *The Journal of Jewish Studies*, vol. 13 (1962), 23-29. For the importance of common meals (*sundeipnon*), even among the Jews of the Dispersion, by the first century BC, cp. Josephus. *Antiquities* 14:214f.
[31] See Strack-Billerbeck, *Kommentar (ut supra)*, excursus 24, 'Ein altjüdisches Gastmahl'.
[32] See Jeremias, *The Eucharistic Words of Jesus, ut supra*, 44-46.

mainly stressed by the first-century sources.[33] In the home, they were unregulated, except by the injunctions and exhortations of the Old Testament to read and meditate continually in God's Law (Deut. 17:19; Josh. 1:8; Ps. 1:2; 119:97) and to teach it to one's children (Gen. 18:19; Deut. 6:7; 11:19; 32:46; Ps. 78:4-7); and the two first-century references that we have to private Bible-reading are both in the context of the teaching of children by their parents (4 Macc. 18:10-19; 2 Tim. 3:15).[34]

In the synagogue on the sabbath, Bible reading and teaching mainly took place at Morning Prayer, and to a lesser degree at Afternoon Prayer, but had no part in Evening or Additional Prayer. This inevitably made Morning Prayer (which also included both the Shema and the Tephillah, not just the latter) the most important service of the sabbath. The basic item was the reading of the Pentateuch, which is attested by the New Testament, Philo and Josephus,[35] and which was read from sabbath to sabbath according to a set order, interrupted only at the seasons of certain holy days (Mishnah Megillah 3:4-6). It appears from the Babylonian Talmud (Megillah 29b) and later evidence that the whole Pentateuch was read in 3 to 3½ years.[36] A reading from the Prophets was added on sabbaths and major holy days (Lk. 4:16-20; Acts 13:15, 27; Mishnah Megillah 4:2), which was chosen according to its suitability to the lection from the Pentateuch, and was not originally a prescribed passage (Lk.

---

33 In every one of the references to the sabbath-day worship of the synagogue collected in note 20, except two of those from Josephus, the theme is Scripture-reading and teaching.

34 If Timothy was brought up by his Greek father and Jewish mother in the town where Paul found him living, and where apparently he was well known (Acts 16:1-3; 20:4), it was one in which there is not known to have been a synagogue; so it was very likely his mother who taught him the Scriptures.

35 Note esp. Acts 13:15; 15:21; Philo, *Hypothetica* 7:12f.; Josephus, *Against Apion* 2:175. There is, in addition, the synagogue inscription from before 70 AD discovered at the Ophel, Jerusalem, which states that the synagogue there had been built 'for the reading of the Law and for the teaching of the commandments' (see E. L. Sukenik, *Ancient Synagogues in Palestine and Greece*, Schweich Lectures, London, British Academy, 1934, 69ff.).

36 As Heinemann shows, the theory of a standard cycle of readings lasting exactly 3 years — whether beginning in Nisan, as Adolph Büchler argued, or in Tishri, as Jacob Mann argued — is contrary to the mediaeval evidence that, even at that date, Palestinian practice varied, and that the cycle might last up to 3½ years ('The Triennial Lectionary Cycle', in *The Journal of Jewish Studies*, vol. 19, 1968, 41-48). Charles Perrot ingeniously conjectures that there was both a precise 3-year cycle beginning in Tishri and a 3½ year cycle beginning in Nisan and Tishri alternately, as well as other customs (*La lecture de la Bible dans la synagogue*, Hildesheim, Gerstenberg, 1973, ch. 7). Perrot holds that the 1-year Babylonian cycle which displaced these Palestinian schemes was devised in the second century AD (173f.). Such recent investigations really make nonsense of the lectionary theories developed, as a supposed background to the gospels, by a succession of New Testament scholars from R. G. Finch to Michael Goulder.

The Centres, Patterns and Elements of Jewish Worship 19

4:16-20; M. Megillah 4:10). At Afternoon Prayer, a portion of the Pentateuch lection for the next sabbath was read, but no reading from the Prophets was added (M. Megillah 3:6-4:1). With the exception of Psalms and of Esther (used at Purim), the Hagiographa was not read at all: it is mentioned by the Babylonian Talmud as a peculiarity of the Jews of Nehardea that they included a reading from the Hagiographa at Afternoon Prayer (Shabbath 116b). One of the reasons given for this omission is significant: 'because of neglect of the beth ha-midrash' (Mishnah Shabbath 16:1). The 'beth ha-midrash' is the 'house of exposition': exposition originally followed the readings at Morning Prayer in the synagogue itself (Lk. 4:20-27; Acts 13:15-41), and a separate hall was later built for this purpose. The exposition might well continue, with inevitable interruptions for the midday meal and other services, throughout the rest of the day (Philo, *Hypothetica* 7:13). Josephus, likewise, quotes evidence from a pagan observer that the Jews appeared to spend the whole sabbath-day in the synagogue (*Against Apion* 1:209).

The synagogue ministry is a subject in itself.[37] By the first century, as was remarked earlier, the synagogue had become a more important teaching-centre than the Temple, and the teaching-duties of the priests had largely been taken over by others. These others were the elders, lawyers, teachers of the Law, scribes (Scripture-experts) or rabbis, as they are variously called in the New Testament. They had studied the Law and the traditions under more senior rabbis, as Paul did under Gamaliel I (Acts 22:3), and probably — in view of New Testament Christian practice — it was already customary for their teacher afterwards to ordain them, by the laying-on of hands. They would then become recognised teachers in the synagogue of the locality where they lived, and would be called upon by the rulers of the synagogue to expound on the sabbath at Morning Prayer, though the rulers could alternatively call upon visiting teachers to do so (Acts 13:15). The only element in the synagogue service which required a priest was the pronouncement of the Aaronic blessing during the Tephillah, for which a priest was necessary in order to conform to Num. 6:23. The synagogue service of Palestine had also a high degree of congregational participation. Quite apart from the congregational Amen's and other responses, any male might apparently be called upon to read the Hebrew Scriptures, supply the Aramaic translation, or recite the Shema or Tephillah: even a minor, a blind man or a man in rags was not wholly excluded from these privileges (Mishnah Megillah 4:4-8).

---

[37] Especially important on this subject is Julius Newman, *Semikhah* (Manchester, The University Press, 1950). On the first-century Jewish priesthood, see Joachim Jeremias, *Jerusalem in the Time of Jesus* (English translation, London, S.C.M., 1969), ch. 8.

III. THE TRANSITION FROM JEWISH WORSHIP TO CHRISTIAN

Having attempted to trace with as much accuracy as possible the state of Jewish worship in the New Testament period, and to avoid the mistakes often made on this subject even by responsible writers, we are in some position to trace the points of continuity and discontinuity with early Christian worship, though this also is less fully attested than one would wish, and is likewise subject to strange misrepresentations.[38] We are trying to see Jewish and Christian worship as a whole, with their natural points of contact, and will aim to avoid the practice of basing claims of dependence on vague and scattered similarities, or of 'augmenting' our knowledge by wild speculation about what is implied in the imagery of the Fourth Gospel or in the account of the heavenly worship (modelled on that of the Temple, not of the Christian congregation) given by the book of Revelation. Even careful and detailed studies, such as Cesare Giraudo's *La struttura letteraria della preghiera eucaristica* (Analecta Biblica 92, Rome, Biblical Institute, 1981) remain less than convincing if they concentrate simply on the very general similarities of form between Jewish prayers and Christian, and do not ponder the occasions on which they were used and the manner of their use.

The centres of worship for Jewish Christians before A.D. 70 were the same as those for other Jews, namely, the Temple, the synagogue and the home. Since, as we have seen, the Jewish Christians attempted to maintain the ordinances of Judaism alongside their Christian counterparts, they doubtless observed the Jewish pattern of worship on weekdays and sabbaths, and on the annual festivals of Judaism as well, and did it in much the same way as other Jews, except where there were Christian truths to witness to. We see traces of this continuance of Jewish observances in Peter and John's visit to the Temple for the afternoon hour of prayer, in Paul's agreement to offer the sacrifice for Jewish Christians who are accomplishing a vow, and in his permission to Jewish Christians to keep Jewish holy days (Acts 3:1; 21:23-26; Rom. 14:5). As long as Jewish Christians were not expelled from the synagogues, and the Temple was still standing, this doubtless remained the custom; and even when they *were* expelled from the synagogues, it was perfectly possible for them

---

[38] Few writers on early Christian worship, sadly, have any proficiency in Jewish studies. Even those who do can make extraordinary mistakes, for example, C. W. Dugmore, who holds that Jews and Christians alike held daily services from New Testament times onward, and that the Hagiographa were read in the synagogue (*The Influence of the Synagogue upon the Divine Office, ut supra*, 14, 111 etc.). Conversely, Jewish writers tend to know little of Christian worship: the most distinguished exception, probably, Eric Werner, shows too little discrimination in the use of Jewish evidence gathered from different ages as illustrative of early Christian practice.

to form Christian synagogues, in much the same way as other groupings of Jews did (Acts 6:9). Their Christian allegiance, however, did not allow them to be content with Jewish worship alone. Their daily visits to the Temple became occasions of evangelistic preaching as well as prayer (Acts 2:46-3:26; 5:42); no doubt the same happened in the synagogue on the sabbath; and to the ordinary observances of the home there was added teaching and the breaking of bread (Acts 2:42, 46; 5:42), augmented, very likely, by various charismatic ministries. Because of the prevailing poverty of the Jerusalem church (Rom. 15:26; Gal. 2:10), which was probably due in part to the high cost of living in Jerusalem,[39] and which caused it special distress in times of world-wide famine (Acts 11:28-30), a high degree of community of goods and especially of food was observed there (Acts 4:32-5:11; 6:1f.), not unlike that practised by the Essenes, who had colonies in many of the cities of Judaea.[40] This was the rather unusual background of the daily agapes-cum-eucharists which the Jerusalem church seems to have held (Acts 2:42, 46), and which were held only weekly in churches less severely afflicted by poverty (Acts 20:7; cp. 1 Cor. 11:7-22); though in both cases the agape took the place of the festal meal at which the eucharist was instituted, and gave the eucharist its own much greater frequency. As the meals were held daily at Jerusalem, they would of course be held on the first day of the week as well as the seventh; and since it is probable that the observance of Sunday originated among the Jewish Christians of Palestine,[41] Christian worship as a whole on that day was probably modelled, from the outset, on sabbath-day worship, though without Additional Prayer (corresponding to the sabbath-day sacrifice exclusively), and using the house-church rather than the synagogue as the meeting place for the other three services. Some confirmation of this is provided by the Christian Tephillah preserved in a fourth-century Syrian compilation, *Apostolic Constitutions* 7:33-38. The Tephillah is in the sabbath-day form, but adapted for use on Sunday; that is to say, it consists of the first three and last three of the eighteen benedictions (though the very last is for some reason omitted), each with its proper theme, but applied in a Christian way; the third duly includes the Kedushah response, and in the authentic Jewish form, according to which Is. 6:3 is followed by Ezk. 3:12; while the

---

[39] See Jeremias, *Jerusalem in the Time of Jesus, ut supra.*, 120-23.

[40] See Philo, *Quod Omnis Probus Liber Sit* 85-87; *Hypothetica* 11:1, 10-13; Josephus, *War* 2:124-27.

[41] See *This is the Day, ut supra*. 31-35. Note especially the Jewish name for Sunday in Acts 20:7, 1 Cor. 16:2; its implied connection with the Jewish week; the other name given to it by the *Didache*, in an Aramaic form; and the observance of Sunday by the less heretical party among the Ebionites.

middle twelve benedictions are replaced, as is customary on the sabbath, by the sabbath benediction, which here does not only speak of the meaning and value of the sabbath, but goes on to speak of the still greater excellence of the Lord's Day.[42] The other important passage of Scripture in the Jewish Tephillah, the Aaronic blessing, is omitted from this Christian form along with the related last benediction; but elsewhere in the work, at *Apostolic Constitutions* 2:57, it is used in a position parallel to the Jewish, at the end of the old eucharistic intercession.

An alternative approach to the Tephillah was to use in its place Jesus's tephillah, the Lord's Prayer. This is what we find in *Didache* 8, where Christians are directed to say the Lord's Prayer three times each day (just as Jews did in the case of the Tephillah). Originally, perhaps, both were said, in accordance with the Jewish-Christian practice of adding Christian observances to Jewish, and hence the Tephillah in the *Apostolic Constitutions*, at which we have been looking; but the *Didache*, though it originated in Palestine or Syria, and probably before A.D. 100, reflects in the very same section the growing antagonism towards the Jews, requiring Christian fast days to be substituted for those of the 'hypocrites'. In a similar way, it substitutes the Lord's Prayer for the Tephillah, and maintains the Lord's Day without mention of the sabbath. No doubt the Lord's Prayer was said individually at the three hours of prayer on weekdays, and corporately on the Lord's Day. Surprisingly, however, the Lord's Prayer does not appear in Christian liturgical texts until a late date. It is not at first found either in the daily offices or in the eucharist. Up to 1971, it was not regularly included in the main Roman offices of morning and evening, Lauds and Vespers (though it was in Terce, Sext and None), and the late date of its introduction into the East Syrian (Nestorian) morning and evening offices is on record.[43] As for use at the eucharist, the Lord's Prayer is not in Hippolytus, which is admittedly not a complete text, but neither is it in the fourth-century Syrian rite (*Apostolic Constitutions*) nor Egyptian rite (Serapion), but is first mentioned in Cyril of Jerusalem's

---

[42] Attention was directed to this Christianized Tephillah by Kaufman Kohler (among others) in his article 'The Origin and Composition of the Eighteen Benedictions', published in 1924 and reproduced in Petuchowski's *Contributions to the Scientific Study of Jewish Liturgy (ut supra)*. The presence of the Kedushah in this Christian Tephillah perhaps accounts for the ancient inclusion of the Sanctus in the ante-communion of Greek liturgies: cp. Joseph Bingham, *The Antiquities of the Christian Church* (Oxford, The University Press, 1855 edn.) 14:2:3.

[43] See Juan Mateos, *Lelya-Sapra: Essai d'interprétation des matines chaldéennes* (Rome, Pont. Inst. Orientalium Studiorum, 1959), 81-83. It was added in reaction to Monophysite criticism. The Lord's Prayer is in the present-day Matins (= Lauds) and Vespers of the Orthodox Church, but evidence for its inclusion does not appear to go back behind the Middle Ages.

Mystagogic Catecheses 5:11-18 and Ambrose's *De Sacramentis* 5:4:24. So it was presumably a recent innovation. How is this to be accounted for? The likely answer lies in the problems which, as we saw, first-century Judaism was having with the three hours of prayer. These led the early Church to adopt the expedient of the Essenes and reduce the hours to two, morning and evening — a tendency no doubt accentuated by the destruction of the Temple, which removed the sacrificial rationale of Afternoon Prayer as a principal hour of prayer, and did the same for Additional Prayer on the sabbath. The Church had now two hours of prayer, observed individually on weekdays and corporately on Sunday — yet the Old Testament spoke of three daily hours of prayer, and the Church itself had been saying the Lord's Prayer three times a day. So three minor hours of prayer were developed, at the third, sixth and ninth hours, which, as Dugmore points out, were ordinary divisions of the day for worldly affairs,[44] and the Lord's Prayer was transferred to those hours. Tertullian (*On Prayer* 25) and Clement of Alexandria (*Stromata* 7:7:40) both attest the existence of these earliest three minor hours at the end of the second century, Tertullian adding that the main hours of prayer are, however, 'at the entrance of day and night'. The hours developed in time into fixed liturgical services, and we duly find the Lord's Prayer used at Terce, Sext and None, but not at Lauds nor (except on Sundays) at Vespers. However, the two main hours of prayer, at the beginning and end of the day, continued to be the two main ones, and for a long time the services of the minor hours were not used corporately except by monks.[45] An absence of the Lord's Prayer from corporate worship was obviously an anomaly, so in the fourth century we begin to see the Lord's Prayer being reintroduced into corporate worship, and this time not in the offices but at the heart of the eucharist.

With the destruction of the Temple and the expulsion of Jewish Christians from the synagogue. their situation became not unlike that of Gentile Christians. In his Gentile mission, Paul had normally begun his work at the synagogue, and tried to build the church round a Jewish nucleus (Acts 9:20; 13:5, 14; 14:1; 17:1f., 10, 17; 18:4, 19; 19:8), only separating the disciples when Jewish opposition forced him to (Acts 19:8f; cp. Acts 13:44-48). There too, probably, the separated Christian congregations at first regarded themselves as 'synagogues', just as the congrega-

---

44 *The Influence of the Synagogue upon the Divine Office, ut supra*, 66f. He appropriately quotes Matt. 20:3, 5 and Tertullian, *On Fasting* 10.
45 See W. J. Grisbrooke, in *The Study of Liturgy, ut supra*, 365f.

tions in Palestine and Syria did,[46] and modelled their worship on what they had been used to in the synagogues, though the prevalence of Greek-speaking Gentile converts caused the original Jewish character of their worship to be 'more rapidly obscured. In both areas, the separated Christian congregations probably met at first in homes (Rom. 16:5; 1 Cor. 16:19; Col. 4:15; Philem. 2), as they had already been doing for purely Christian purposes (Acts 2:46; 12:12), or else in borrowed halls (Acts 19:9); and then, when numbers demanded and absence of persecution permitted it, they started buying or building synagogues or churches of their own.

As for those purely Jewish observances which Jewish Christians maintained, Gentile Christians had been exempted from them almost from the outset (Acts 15:1-35); and after the destruction of the Temple Jewish Christians also, probably, discarded them at an increasing rate, as the *Didache* indicates.

THE CHRISTIAN MINISTRY OF THE WORD

Since the Tephillah has left its traces on Christian worship, one would certainly expect the more ancient Shema to have done the same. So indeed it has, but the evidence is disputed, and can more satisfactorily be presented later, after other relevant evidence has been surveyed. Another reasonable expectation is that the Scriptures would be read and expounded at the Sunday morning service, as at the sabbath morning service in the synagogue; and few practices of the early Church are in fact better attested than this. The earliest witness to it is Justin Martyr at Rome in the mid-second century, who says that at the Sunday morning ante-communion

'the memoirs of the apostles or the writings of the prophets are read, as long as time permits; then, when the reader has ceased, the president verbally instructs, and exhorts to the imitation of these good things' (*First Apology* 67).

Here Christian Scriptures can be read as an alternative to Jewish. In Syria, however, they were treated as additional: in *Apostolic Constitutions* 2:57 there are two readings from the Old Testament at this service, and two, apparently, from the New, the Psalms of David being sung between the Testaments; and after all the lections, a series of sermons follows. As in Judaism, evidently, the morning service was no short one!

---

[46] See *Shepherd* of Hermas (Mandate 11), and Justin Martyr, *Dialogue with Trypho* 63, written at Rome and Ephesus respectively. For the use of the term by Christians in Palestine and Syria, cp. Jam. 2:2; Ignatius, *To Polycarp* 4; Theophilus, *To Autolycus* 2:14.

The closest parallel of all to Jewish practice is provided by the East Syrian (Nestorian) liturgy, where the two Old Testament readings are normally (and especially on Sundays) a reading from the Pentateuch and a reading from the Prophets.[47] It is true that the 'prophetic' reading is occasionally taken from the Hagiographa, but this is because the Syrian and Palestinian Church, as far back as records go, was impelled, by the important testimony to Christ found in books like Psalms, Job, Proverbs and Daniel, to modify drastically the Jewish rule against the liturgical reading of the Hagiographa.[48] The Psalms were sung, not just read, but they too were used more freely by the early Church than in the synagogue, where it appears that only the Hallel (Pss. 113-118) was used, and this only on festivals (Mishnah Sukkah 3:9-11, Rosh ha-Shanah 4:7); whereas in the above passage from the *Apostolic Constitutions* we see Psalms being used every Sunday, and the practice may go back to New Testament times (1 Cor. 14:26; Eph. 5:19; Col. 3:16). It was hardly influenced, however, by the use of the Hallel at the Passover meal (Mk. 14:26; Mishnah Pesahim 10:5-7), since this was only a festal usage once a year. Moreover, Psalms were used, as we shall see, at the agape. The whole Psalter was also to be recited, ultimately, in the daily offices, through monastic influence; and this too goes back to tenuous Jewish beginnings. For the fixed use of Pss. 148-150 at the old Roman Lauds, which is also found in Nestorian and Orthodox Matins, appears to be connected with a Jewish practice mentioned by Rabbi Jose in the Babylonian Talmud (Shabbath 118b) of saying the last six Psalms every day. This was a devotion of pious individuals which, having been brought into the Christian Church, was eventually given liturgical form in the daily morning office, both among Jews and among Christians.[49]

The teaching office in the local Christian congregation was assigned to men who bore the same title as the teachers in the synagogue, that of 'elder' (Gk. *presbuteros*), and who have borne it ever since. The 'elders' of Acts 20:28; 1 Tim. 5:17; Tit. 1:9, have teaching responsibilities (like those of the Jewish 'elders' in Philo, *Hypothetica* 7:13), as well as the responsibility of ruling *i.e.*, of pastoral oversight. They are not simply called by God but outwardly appointed (Acts 14:23; Tit; 1:5), apparently

---

[47] See A. J. Maclean, *East Syrian Daily Offices* (London, Rivington, Percival & Co., 1894), 264-281.

[48] See *Apostolic Constitutions* 2:57; F. C. Burkitt, 'The Early Syriac Lectionary System', in *Proceedings of the British Academy*, 10, 1921-23, 301-338; and, for evidence from Palestine, Cyril of Jerusalem, *Catecheses* 4:35; Athanase Renoux, ed., *Le codex arménien Jérusalem 121* (Patrologia Orientalis 35, 36).

[49] See Anton Baumstark, *Comparative Liturgy* (English translation, London, Mowbray, 1958), 37f. Baumstark's account is somewhat speculative, however.

by the laying-on of hands (Acts 6:6; 1 Tim. 4:14; 5:22; 2 Tim. 1:6), which was also the original Jewish mode of appointment (Tosephta Sanhedrin 1:1). The abundance of spiritual gifts in the early Church meant that the congregational participation practised in the synagogue was maintained and indeed excelled: in 1 Cor. 14, not only is the congregational Amen mentioned, but many lay Christians are found helping to lead the service — in Paul's eyes *too* many, it may be, for the service lacks 'decency' and 'order'. The tendency to institutionalization, as well as the proper requirement of order, was destined to check this every-member ministry, and by the end of the second century we find Tertullian attributing priestly titles to the ordained ministry, which acted as a further check (*On Prescription* 41; *On the Veiling of Virgins* 9). The subject of the Christian ministry cannot, of course, be carried further here.

THE ORIGIN OF THE SUNDAY EUCHARIST

The background of the eucharist, as virtually all the great Christian students of Judaism maintain (Edersheim, Dalman, Strack-Billerbeck and the rest), and as Jeremias has maintained at length most recently,[50] was the Passover meal. It is impossible and unnecessary to rehearse all the arguments here. Suffice it to say that the Synoptic Gospels teach this, and that the main evidence to the contrary is Jn. 18:28. The independent historical value of the Fourth Gospel has been increasingly stressed by modern New Testament study, but this does not necessarily imply an ignorance, in its writer, of the synoptic tradition; and if, on the contrary, the writer assumes a knowledge of the synoptic tradition, this would probably make it possible for him to use the phrase 'eat the passover' in the broad sense suggested by Deut. 16:2f., as referring to all the feasting of the week of Unleavened Bread, without fear of being misunderstood. How the events of the Last Supper fit into the pattern of the Passover meal as set out in the Mishnah (Pesahim 10) is very lucidly explained by Strack-Billerbeck.[51] The only significant discrepancy is that Jesus seems to have interpreted the items on the Passover table at various points in the meal,

---

[50] In *The Eucharistic Words of Jesus (ut supra)*

[51] *Kommentar, ut supra*, excursus 4, 'Das Passahmahl'. David Daube's contention that the Passover meal must have been rearranged after the time of the Mishnah, since the questions and answers about its meaning would not naturally come until towards the end of the meal (*The New Testament and Rabbinic Judaism*, London, Athlone Press, 1956, 186-195), is hardly convincing. Since the questions and answers all relate to items of food, they would be appropriate as soon as the table was laid. Equally unconvincing is D. Cohn-Sherbok's strange article 'A Jewish Note on ΤΟ ΠΟΤΗΡΙΟΝ ΤΗΣ ΕΥΛΟΓΙΑΣ' in *New Testament Studies*, vol. 27 (1980-81), 704-09, which confuses hymns and benedictions.

as they came into use, not all together, and without being prompted by the son of the household's questions; but even in the time of the Mishnah the form of the interpretation was not fixed (Pesahim 10:5), and the absence of the questions is probably simply due to the absence of children, whose presence may not have been normal up to A.D. 70, when the celebration still involved a pilgrimage to Jerusalem.[52]

It is important to realize that, at the Last Supper, the eucharist was in two parts (the first 'as they were eating', Mt. 26:26; Mk. 14:22, and the second 'after supper', Lk. 22:20; 1 Cor. 11:25), and that the two were integral to the Passover meal. The breaking of the bread, with its grace, and the Common Grace over the third cup ('the cup of the blessing'), would have been there anyway, and so would the accompanying acts of taking and distributing: such acts are regularly found in accounts of Jewish meals at this period, examples being the miraculous feedings in the gospels (Mk. 6:41; 8:6f.), the meal just before Paul's shipwreck (Acts 27:35) and the Passover meal as described in the Mishnah (Pesahim 10). Even interpretative words would have been used at the Passover meal: what was new was that in connection with the bread and the third cup Jesus gave an entirely unconventional interpretation, concerned with his own sacrificial death, and in each case commanded that what he had said and done in relation to that particular item of the meal should be repeated (Lk. 22:19; 1 Cor. 11:24f.). At first, what he had instituted was repeated as two parts of a large meal — the agape or 'love feast' which, evidently for the benefit of the poorer Christians at Jerusalem and elsewhere (cp. 1 Cor. 11:17-22), took the place of the Passover meal, but was held daily or weekly, not annually. The eucharist was quite early separated from the agape, perhaps because the latter became an occasion not of love but of selfishness and strife, as at Corinth; but they are still combined in I Cor. 11, in *Didache* 9f. (as the phrase 'after you are satisfied' indicates) and in *Epistle of the Apostles* 15 (probably an Egyptian text). This takes us up to about A.D. 125. There has been much discussion, largely pointless, on the question whether, while still combined, the eucharist follows the agape or the agape the eucharist, as if they were two different things (and on such an assumption the graces of the *Didache* have sometimes been supposed to be merely 'agape-graces'): actually, the eucharist was part, or rather two parts, of the agape — those parts in connection with which our Lord's unique interpretative words were said — and the two parts were probably often at separate points in the meal, as on the occasion of the Last Supper. Nor need they always have been at the same

---

[52] See J. B. Segal, *The Hebrew Passover from the Earliest Times to A.D. 70* (London, O.U.P., 1963), 254, 257f., etc.

points. Though, at a Jewish dinner party, the breaking of the bread usually came first and the first cup of wine afterwards, there were other cups of wine later, and if there was an entrée, as at the Passover meal, the first cup of wine would precede this and so would come before the breaking of the bread.[53] Hence, no doubt, the first cup in the (longer) Lukan account of the Last Supper (Lk. 22:17); and hence, very likely, the reversal of the order of the bread and cup in the *Didache* (where the first cup and not the third has become the sacramental one), and the difference between the two texts of the *Epistle of the Apostles*, in one of which the agape (presumably beginning with an entrée) is mentioned before the eucharist, and in the other of which the eucharist is mentioned before the agape.

Since, as we saw, the Jews had their main meal of the day in the evening, it was natural for the agape to be held at this time of day, as indeed the Last Supper had been. When, in 1 Cor. 11:20, Paul calls the combined meal 'the Lord's Supper' (*kuriakon deipnon*), he is probably indicating that it was still held at this hour. Evening Prayer, observed corporately in the Gentile churches on the Lord's Day alone, since they did not observe sabbaths (Col. 2:16f.), was of course also held at this hour, and when prolonged by the unconventional addition of preaching it might postpone the meal into the night, as in Acts 20:7-12; but the Passover meal also was held after nightfall, so Paul would not have thought this anomalous.[54] *Didache* 14 speaks as if the combined meal is the first event of the Lord's Day, so it may be that in the Semitic circles to which the author is writing it was regularly held after nightfall, like the Passover meal, nightfall on Saturday being regarded as the beginning of Sunday. Again, when Pliny the Younger describes the Sunday worship of the Christians of Bithynia about A.D. 112 as consisting of two services, the second of them a meal (*Epistle* 10:96), he is probably speaking of a meal in the afternoon or evening, this being the time of the main meal among the Greeks and Romans, and evening being the time of the second Christian hour of worship as soon as they reduced the hours from three to two. In *Epistle of the Apostles* 15, the meal is said to be held as late as cockrow (03.00hrs.), but this is apparently a peculiarity of Eastertide, derived, according to Jeremias, from a Jewish-Christian practice of

---

53 See Strack-Billerbeck, *Kommentar, ut supra,* excursus 4 and 24.
54 I am assuming, on the grounds that daybreak is described as 'on the morrow' (verses 7, 11), that this service took place on the evening that ended Sunday, not on the evening that began Sunday; indeed, the author of Acts may be thinking of the day as beginning at daybreak rather than at nightfall, as he does in Acts 4:3, 23:32.

fasting during the Jewish Passover meal,[55] but more likely prompted by the apparent hour of the resurrection (Lk. 24:1; Jn. 20:1). It implies, like the *Didache*, a reckoning whereby Sunday begins at nightfall, and such a reckoning did in fact continue in the Egyptian church for centuries (see Cassian, *Institutes* 2:18).

THE ORIGIN OF THE EUCHARISTIC THANKSGIVING PRAYER

When the eucharist and agape were separated, it was natural for the eucharist to be moved to the morning. This is probably nothing to do with the Roman prohibition of clubs,[56] which would have abolished rather than changed the hour of the eucharist, and which did not even abolish the agape: the agape was still important enough in A.D. 692 to need regulating by canon 74 of the Quinisext Council. Rather, if the eucharist was to be moved away from the hour of the evening meal and evening service, the hour of the morning service was the one obvious time to which it could be moved, and a time of great significance too, since, in addition to the usual items of prayer and thanksgiving, corresponding to the Tephillah and Shema, the Scriptures were read and expounded then. This development brought together for the first time the full ante-communion and eucharist, as we see them at Rome about A.D. 155 in Justin Martyr (*First Apology* 67). At the Sunday morning service he describes, there are Scripture readings, a sermon and a prayer, just as at Jewish Morning Prayer on the sabbath, after which the eucharist follows. We learn from ch. 65 that the prayer is wide in scope and petitionary in character, like the Tephillah, though concerned with the Church instead of Israel, and that it precedes the eucharist even when the lections and sermon are replaced by a baptism. This close bond with the eucharist probably indicates that it was already used with the eucharist at the former evening hour when, on the Jewish pattern, the Tephillah would likewise have been said. What is missing is the Shema, which, to judge from synagogue practice, one would also expect to find at the morning and evening hour. Or is it missing? For an important effect of separating the eucharist from the agape was to bring the two parts of the eucharist together, so that the benediction over the bread and the Common Grace over the cup (and the separate benediction over the wine as well, if the items were reversed, as in the *Didache*) coalesced in a single thanksgiving prayer. This has already happened in Justin Martyr. Now, the Shema also, it must be remembered, was according to Josephus basically a

---

[55] *The Eucharistic Words of Jesus, ut supra*, 216f.
[56] As Willy Rordorf supposes (*Sunday*, English translation, London S.C.M., 1968, 250-53).

thanksgiving, the themes of its benedictions being creation, revelation and redemption. The earliest form that we have of the single thanksgiving prayer at the eucharist is that of the Roman church, only vaguely described by Justin, but quoted in full in Hippolytus's *Apostolic Tradition* 4 (about A.D. 215), where the opening themes for thanksgiving are precisely creation, revelation and redemption *through Christ* (though the order is not strictly observed).[57] The prayer goes on, in the institution narrative, to give thanks for the institution of the eucharist, thus combining with the themes of the Shema the themes of the two or more graces here replaced — namely wine, bread and food (the thanksgiving for the land and the prayer for Israel and Jerusalem in the second and third benedictions of the Common Grace being omitted, as obsolete, or as covered by the earlier prayer for the Church). That this was the original function of the institution narrative is indicated by three facts:

(i). that in Hippolytus, as in the Syrian and Byzantine liturgies (but not in most of the later Western liturgies or in the Egyptian liturgies, where a petition for consecration has been intruded before it),[58] the institution narrative is itself the last of the themes of thanksgiving.

(ii). that in Sarapion the institution narrative includes the petition about the bread scattered on the mountains from the grace over the bread in *Didache* 9 (Sarapion is the earliest surviving form of the Egyptian institution narrative: in the Dêr-Balizeh Papyrus the petition has been moved to a more 'natural' position, immediately after the petition for consecration, and in the Liturgy of St. Mark it has been dropped altogether).[59]

(iii). that in the East Syrian (Nestorian) Liturgy of Addai and Mari there is no institution narrative: this at least suggests that the earlier part

---

[57] Justin describes the prayer as consisting of 'prayers and thanksgivings', as giving 'praise and glory to the Father of the universe through the name of the Son and of the Holy Spirit', as giving 'thanks at considerable length for our being counted worthy to receive these things at his hands', and as 'the prayer of the form of words which is from him (Jesus)' (*First Apology* 65-67). All these four phrases fit Hippolytus's prayer, and the last two appear to allude to the institution narrative, appended in Hippolytus to the other thanksgivings. On the right mode of construing the fourth of the above phrases, see G. J. Cuming, Δι' Ευχης Λογου, in *The Journal of Theological Studies*, n.s. 31, 1980, 80-82.

[58] This is true, regrettably, even of the new Roman canons (two of them based on Hippolytus and the Liturgy of St. Basil!), as it is of recent Anglican revisions also.

[59] See C. H. Roberts and B. Capelle, *An Early Euchologium: the Dêr-Balizeh Papyrus Enlarged and Re-edited* (Bibliothèque du Muséon 23, Louvain, Bureau du Muséon, 1949).

of the great thanksgiving and the institution narrative were drawn from two different sources.[60]

The first two of these facts, though not the third, could also be used in support of Louis Ligier's proposal, in his article 'The Origins of the Eucharistic Prayer' (first published in *Questions Liturgiques* and translated into English in *Studia Liturgica*, vol. 9, 1973, 161-185), that the institution narrative originated as a festal addition to the Common Grace. But, even assuming that this addition *was* made in the first century at Passover, which is quite possible, it would have been made *only* at Passover, and as soon as the eucharist was brought into weekly or daily use — *i.e.,* at once — it would have been dropped. Dr. Ligier's article contains an excellent critical survey of earlier literature on eucharistic origins, notably the writings of Lietzmann, Dix and Bouyer, but his own hypothesis can hardly be correct.

The rest of Hippolytus's prayer can easily be explained, in principle at least, as soon as the great thanksgiving and institution narrative are explained. The anamnesis, stating that we are here and now remembering Christ and carrying out his institution, naturally follows on from the institution narrative; and the epiclesis, praying for the grace of the sacrament, is equally natural, especially when one recalls that it is the only petition which the prayer contains, and that the combination of thanksgiving with petition was frequent in Jewish liturgy and occurred in the Common Grace itself. Why the anamnesis takes the form of an oblation and the petition the form of an epiclesis are, of course, much more difficult questions, and one can here only express the opinion that they are due to Christian causes rather than Jewish. As to the final doxology, it corresponds to the 'seal' of a Jewish benediction, and will be examined in the discussion of prayer-forms at the end of this article. Hippolytus's prayer contains no intercessions, and since these existed separately both Rome (cp. Justin Martyr, *First Apology* 65, 67) and in Syria (cp. *Apostolic Constitutions* 2:57; 8:9-11), in a manner congruous to Jewish practice, the duplication of them in the consecration prayer is probably a secondary development, though perhaps growing out of an early Syrian petition for the Church. The brief petition in question immediately follows the epiclesis in the (Nestorian) Liturgy of Addai and Mari and the older recension of the Liturgy of St. Basil, and may correspond to the

---

[60] For the texts referred to in these three paragraphs, see especially F. E. Brightman and C. Hammond, ed., *Liturgies Eastern and Western* (Oxford, Clarendon Press, 1965 reprint); Cipriano Vagaggini, *The Canon of the Mass and Liturgical Reform* (English translation, London, Chapman, 1967).

third part of the Common Grace, the prayer for Israel and Jerusalem, which *Didache* 10, as we shall see, applies to the Church.[61]

How much the Shema has affected Hippolytus's thanksgiving prayer is shown by comparing it with the three graces in the *Didache*, which are simply related to the Jewish benedictions over wine and over bread, and to the Common Grace. In the *Didache*, the Jewish benedictions are indeed reinterpreted, so as to give thanks for spiritual blessings as well as material — 'life', 'knowledge', 'faith', 'immortality', 'spiritual food and drink'; and the Common Grace, which is still in three parts — each ending 'Thine is the (power and the) glory for ever and ever' — is rearranged, with the benediction for the land replaced, as being obsolete, and the petition for Israel and Jerusalem applied to the Church. And yet the contrast between these Christianized graces and the later Christian consecration prayer is striking. In particular, there is no account here of the historical course of redemption through Christ, such as we find in Hippolytus, and the probable origin of this is the culminating benediction of the Shema, which gives a long historical account of the redemption from Egypt at the Exodus, likewise in the form of a thanksgiving. What is more, the first benediction of the Shema, for creation, to which the Kedushah (beginning with Is. 6:3) is the response, is directly paralleled in the consecration prayers of the old Syrian liturgies. Here the Sanctus comes after the thanksgiving for creation (to which the *Apostolic Constitutions* adds an account of Old Testament history) and before the thanksgiving for revelation and redemption. The thanksgiving for revelation is somewhat attenuated, but the pattern seems clear, alike in *Apostolic Constitutions* 8:12, the Liturgy of St. James, the older recension of the Liturgy of St. Basil and the Liturgy of Addai and Mari.[62] If it be asked why there is no comparable Sanctus in Hippolytus, the likely answer is that the Kedushah in the Shema, though probably ancient, may not be quite as ancient as that in the Tephillah;[63] and this would mean that, although it had appeared at the fountain-head of Jewish liturgy, in Palestine and Syria,

---

[61] This correspondence is plausibly proposed by G. J. Cuming in *He Gave Thanks* (Grove Liturgical Study 28, Bramcote, Grove Books, 1981, 6). The older recension of the Liturgy of St. Basil is the Alexandrian recension: see J. Doresse and E. Lanne, *Un témoin archaïque de la liturgie copte de S. Basile* (Bibliothèque du Muséon 47, Louvain, Publications Universitaires, 1960). The original home of this liturgy is, however, Basil's see of Caesarea in Cappadocia, and it reflects the influence of neighbouring Antioch in Syria.

[62] The magnificent Sanctus in the Liturgy of Addai and Mari appears to be an early addition (see below), but its position is still significant.

[63] See Heinemann, *Prayer in the Talmud, ut supra*, 230-33.

by the beginning of the Christian era,[64] it had not yet been introduced at Rome.[65]

Other possible traces of the influence of the Shema in early Christian worship are provided by the *Didache* and Pliny. The Shema, it will be recalled, includes a group of passages from the Law of Moses, notably the Great Commandment, which in ancient times was preceded by the Decalogue. Now, the opening three sections of the *Didache* group together (with some elaboration) the Great Commandment, the Second Commandment like it, and the Decalogue, as 'the way of life'; and the fourth section concludes:

> 'Thou shalt never forsake the commandments of the Lord, but shalt keep those things which thou hast received, neither adding to them nor taking away from them. In church thou shalt confess thy transgressions, and shalt not betake thyself to prayer with an evil conscience. This is the way of life'.

The requirement of confession is repeated in section 14, as a preparation for the eucharist, so it may be due to Paul's warning about the peril of unworthy participation (1 Cor. 11:27-34). Possibly, in view of section 4, it was preceded by a recitation of the commandments, drawn largely from the Shema, with the merely ceremonial ones omitted. Stronger evidence of this is provided by Pliny's letter, where he says that the Christians of Bithynia

---

64 The apparent existence of Syrian consecration prayers without a Sanctus might suggest that the Kedushah in the Shema was not universal even in Syria. An alternative possibility, however, is that such prayers originated in the benediction for redemption alone, or in the benedictions for revelation and redemption, in which case the Kedushah (attached to the benediction for creation) would not be involved. The arguments used to show that the Sanctus is not original in the Liturgy of Addai and Mari (notably that the succeeding part of the thanksgiving is addressed to Christ not the Trinity, and that the linking phrases after the Sanctus are missing from the related Maronite Anaphora of St. Peter) throw doubt on the originality of the thanksgiving for creation, as well as that of the Sanctus appended to it. The other liturgy without a Sanctus, the Anaphora of St. Epiphanius, certainly does not have a thanksgiving for creation; and if this liturgy originated at Epiphanius's see of Salamis, it was within the area of the influence of Antioch. See E. C. Ratcliff, 'The Original Form of the Anaphora of Addai and Mari', in *The Journal of Theological Studies*, 30, 1928-29, 23-32; Bernard Botte, 'Problèmes de l'anaphore syrienne des apôtres Addaï et Mari', in *L'Orient Syrien*, 10, 1965, 89-106; 'Fragments d'une anaphore inconnue attribuée à S. Epiphane', in *Le Muséon*, 73, 1960, 311-15.

65 With regard to E. C. Ratcliff's theory that the Sanctus originally came at the end of Hippolytus's consecration prayer, which he deduced from supposed Syrian evidence, see the reply by B. D. Spinks, 'A note on the Anaphora outlined in Narsai's Homily XXXII', in *The Journal of Theological Studies*, n.s. 31, 1980, 82-93. Ratcliff may be right in inferring from early Western references to Is. 6:3 that it was already employed liturgically, but we have seen that the Christian Tephillah contained it, so the consecration prayer is not the only place where it can have been used.

'bound themselves by a solemn oath, not to any wicked deeds, but never to commit any fraud, theft or adultery, never to falsify their word, nor deny a trust when they should be called upon to deliver it up'.

This could well reflect a paraphrase of parts of the Decalogue, and the 'solemn oath' could be the 'taking upon oneself the yoke of the kingdom of heaven' and 'the yoke of the commandments', which the use of the Shema was understood to imply (Mishnah Berakoth 2:2). It is true that Pliny is speaking of the morning service not the evening service, as the *Didache* probably is, but the Shema was used by the Jews at both.

A further consideration is that the reason why the Decalogue was dropped from the Jewish Shema — which we saw was 'the insinuations of the heretics' — probably implies that the heretics (*i.e.*, the Christians) were themselves reciting, and not just emphasizing, it. Why they too ceased reciting it, as they must early have done, is a thought-provoking question. Their related confession must also have been early dropped, for in the paraphrase of the *Didache* included in the *Apostolic Constitutions* the words 'in the church' are omitted at the first mention of it, and at the second mention it is changed from a confession into a thanksgiving (*Ap. Const.*, 7:14, 30).

Lastly, in *Apostolic Constitutions* 8:38f., one finds the first and third of the morning benedictions of the Shema, Christianized and considerably altered but still recognizable, and the previous chapter prescribes that they be said at the morning hour of prayer every day (just as the Shema was).

THE ORIGIN OF THE SUNDAY EVENING SERVICE

The transference of the eucharist to Sunday morning left at the evening hour the agape, combined with elements of Jewish Evening Prayer. Justin makes no mention of it, perhaps not thinking it important enough, as never having contained a formal ministry of the word, and now not containing a ministry of the sacrament either. That it did not occur at Rome is not a necessary conclusion to draw, as is often supposed. Certainly, either in Rome or in North Africa the agape took place on the evening of 'a solemn day' (Sunday), as is indicated by Minucius Felix, *Octavius* 9, a work related to Tertullian's *Apology* and probably written before or soon after the end of the second century. Tertullian, *Apology* 39, gives an account of the meal, confirming that it was for the benefit of the poor, stating that it began and ended with grace, and speaking of the bringing in of lights, followed by the singing of hymns, either from the Bible or newly composed. Those from the Bible were doubtless mainly Psalms, and Hippolytus, writing some twenty years later at Rome, speaks of the use of the Hallelujah Psalms (Pss. 104-06, 111-13, 115-117, 135, 146-150) at the agape, adding that the people are to respond 'Hallelujah' (*Apostolic Tradition* 25). *Apostolic Constitutions* 2:57 states that, in the psalm-singing at the ante-communion, the people are to join in at the ends of the verses, but Hippolytus shows they joined in with a Jewish response (cp. Mishnah Sukkah 3:10f., Sotah 5:4). Hippolytus also records the benediction said at the bringing in of the lights (*ibid.*), which we saw was a Jewish custom on the evening that began Sunday. It must have been transferred by Gentile Christians to the evening that ended Sunday, and later to weekday evenings, for in Hippolytus the agape, though still called 'the Lord's Supper', has been moved to weekdays — days suitable for fasting (*Ap. Trad.* 23, 27). The benediction he records interprets light Christologically. It is very similar to the old Greek Vesper-hymn *Phos hilaron* ('Hail, gladdening Light'), and was probably its source.

THE ORIGIN OF THE DAILY SERVICES

The gradual decay of the agape, and its removal to any weekday, left behind on Sunday evenings just the elements of Evening Prayer. Other changes, however, were already taking place. The hours of daily private prayer, augmented already by three minor hours to five, are further augmented in Hippolytus (*Ap. Trad.* 35, 41) and *Apostolic Constitutions* 8:32, 34 to seven or six, and in the monasteries finally became eight. An influential factor here was probably Ps. 119:164, 'seven times a day do I praise thee', taken literally; but as the hours were at three-hourly intervals, it was inevitable that asceticism should want to continue the pattern throughout the whole day and night, making eight in all. A further, and concurrent, development was that the two principal hours, at the beginning and end of the day, became corporate services, on weekdays and not just on Sundays: this has happened to Morning Prayer in Hippolytus (*Ap. Trad.* 39, 41) and to Evening Prayer as well in *Apostolic Constitutions* 2:59; 8:32, 34-39. A parallel development was occurring in Judaism: if A. Z. Idelsohn is right, the three daily hours of prayer in Judaism had become corporate daily services by about A.D. 100. He regards this as one of the trends brought to its completion by Rabban Gamaliel II.[66] Whether it had already started happening before the breach between Church and Synagogue was complete one cannot actually be sure, but the ground had been prepared for it, perhaps unconsciously, in two ways, namely:

    (i). The hours of prayer, and the actual prayers used, on the sabbath

---

[66] *Jewish Liturgy and its Development* (New York, Sacred Music Press, 1932), xviiif., 27f., 118f.

corporately and on weekdays individually, were the same, though items were added on the sabbath. This also appears to be true of the early Church, though with Sunday taking the place of the sabbath.

(ii). Already in Temple times, as we saw earlier, lay *maamads* (or embryo congregations) met on weekdays in selected synagogues in the two, or sometimes three, weeks of the year when the corresponding priestly course was serving in Jerusalem (Mishnah Bikkurim 3:2, Taanith 4:1-5, Megillah 3:4-6); and the Mishnah also speaks of services in some synagogues on Mondays and Thursdays (Megillah 1:3; 3:6-4:1).

The ground being thus prepared, the precipitating cause in the case of Judaism was probably the reorganization necessary after the calamity of A.D. 70, and the tendency to institutionalization which it brought; while in the case of the Church the precipitating causes appear from Hippolytus to have been the need of the clergy for a rule of life and the need of the laity for instruction (*Ap. Trad.* 39, 41), though institutionalization was doubtless a factor here also.

The form of these earliest daily offices doubtless gives some indication of the form of the private devotions which they replaced. In Hippolytus the form is prayer and instruction, for which the private substitute, when necessary, is prayer and Bible-reading. In *Apostolic Constitutions* 8:32, 34, instruction at Morning Prayer, and the private substitute of reading, are also mentioned, but the shape of the liturgical service is given in chapters 35-39 (cp. bk. 2, ch. 59) as follows:

The singing of the morning psalm (Ps. 63).
The bidding prayer from the Sunday eucharist (corresponding in function, though not form, to the Tephillah), with a special concluding collect.
The first of the morning benedictions of the Shema (Christianized).
The third of the morning benedictions of the Shema (Christianized).
The Dismissal.

The shape of the evening service is parallel to this:

The singing of the evening psalm (Ps. 141) at the lighting of the lamps.
The bidding prayer from the Sunday eucharist, with a corresponding concluding collect, perhaps derived from the fourth of the evening benedictions of the Shema (and further adapted, above, for the morning service).[67]
A thanksgiving, perhaps derived from the first of the evening benedictions of the Shema.
A blessing of the congregation by the bishop.
The Dismissal.

---

[67] The morning and evening collects are certainly closely connected, and as the *Apostolic Constitutions* puts the evening service first, it is credible that the former is based on the latter.

The links with Jewish worship at the same hours are here very apparent. So are the links with Sunday worship. In time, however, due to monastic influence, the morning office (Lauds, or eastern Matins) diverged further from the ante-communion and became an independent service, while the evening office (Vespers) remained the same service on Sundays and week-days. Presumably the ante-communion, which from the outset incorporated unique features, was more resistant to monastic changes.[68]

THE ORIGIN OF CHRISTIAN PRAYER-FORMS

Looking back upon the prayers which we have surveyed, it is possible to make a few general reflections about Jewish and Christian benedictions, as regards their similarities and differences of form. A formal comparison is attempted by J. P. Audet in his article 'Esquisse historique du genre littéraire de la «bénédiction» juive et de l'«eucharistie» chrétienne',[69] where he draws attention to the Old Testament benediction formula 'Blessed be the Lord, who . . .' (Gen. 24:27; Ex. 18:10; I Kings 8:15ff. etc.), a formula also echoed in the New Testament Epistles (2 Cor. 1:3f.; Eph. 1:3ff.; 1 Pet. 1:3ff.). Heinemann pays tribute to Audet's study, but points out that the benedictions of the Jewish liturgy regularly address God in the second person, instead of referring to him in the third, and so begin 'Blessed art thou, O Lord our God'. Indeed, in Jewish liturgy the second person is practically reserved for God.[70] In Christian prayers similarly, both in the New Testament period and later, God is addressed in the second person (except for purely literary prayers like those in the Epistles, mentioned above). At Qumran alone are both persons used.

A second point to note is that, in New Testament Greek, to 'bless' (*eulogein*) God and to 'give thanks' (*eucharistein*) to God are interchangeable expressions. This is clear from 1 Cor. 14:16 and from the accounts of the graces at the miraculous feedings and the Last Supper (cp. Mk. 6:41 with 8:6, and Mk. 14:22 with 14:23; Lk. 22:19; 1 Cor. 11:24). In Semitic languages also, such an interchange is possible. The Qumran *Hymns* occasionally begin 'Blessed art thou, O Lord', but normally 'I thank thee, O Lord/God'. Christian thanksgivings, starting with those of Christ himself (Matt. 11:25; Jn. 11:41), show a like preference for the form 'I/we thank thee'. This is how all the graces in *Didache*

---

[68] Dugmore gives a different explanation of how this came about (*The Influence of the Synagogue upon the Divine Office, ut supra,* 57f.), but his account is vitiated by his assumption that daily corporate services existed in the Church from the beginning.

[69] In *Revue Biblique,* 65, 1958, 371-399.

[70] *Prayer in the Talmud, ut supra,* chs. 3, 4. There are early examples of such benedictions in the Apocrypha (Song of the Three 2-22; 1 Macc. 4:30-33).

9f. begin (whereas their Pharisaic counterparts would have begun 'Blessed art thou'); and the same is true of Hippolytus's consecration prayer. One of the benedictions of the Christianized Tephillah begins 'Blessed art thou, O Lord, King of the ages' (*Apostolic Constitutions* 7:34), but such a form is rare in Christian liturgy.

A third point is that, in transposing a prayer from Hebrew into Greek, a series of participles will become a series of relative clauses. Nothing is more striking in Hippolytus's consecration prayer, and derived prayers, than the long series of relative clauses which they contain: but comparable series of participles may be found in benedictions of the Shema and Tephillah.

A fourth point is that in Christian prayer, following the almost invariable practice of Jesus himself and his model-prayer for his disciples, God is customarily addressed as 'Father', and not simply as 'Lord' or 'God', as in Jewish prayer. This is another distinctive feature of the graces in the *Didache*; and the Fatherhood of God is implied in Christian prayers, even where it is not directly expressed, often by referring to Jesus in the third person or as God's Son (cp. Acts 4:27, 30 and Hippolytus's consecration prayer). The title 'Father' for God is by no means unknown in Jewish liturgy, where it goes back to the Old Testament teaching that God is the Father of Israel (Deut. 32:6; Is. 63:16; 64:8); but Jesus's sense of his unique Sonship, and his sharing of this privilege with his followers, has made the address 'Father' much more characteristic of Christian liturgy.

A fifth point is that, as we saw earlier, Jewish benedictions are normally 'sealed' by an individualized ending, in which God is blessed for his willingness to grant the particular benefit which has been requested, or for which he has been thanked, or is blessed under the character which has been ascribed to him in praise, in the course of the benediction. The seal is often all that justifies the name 'benediction' when the benediction is really petitionary, but in other cases it sums up the thanksgivings or praises that have been offered. There is one seal of this sort in the Christianized Tephillah: 'Blessed art thou for ever, O thou great Protector of the posterity of Abraham' (*Apostolic Constitutions* 7:33). In each of the graces of *Didache* 9f., however, one standard seal is used: 'Thine is the glory for ever and ever'. It is used four times in precisely that form, but is twice expanded, either to 'Thine is the glory and the power through Jesus Christ for ever and ever' or to 'Thine is the power and the glory for ever and ever'. In this last form it is also added as a seal to the Lord's Prayer (*Didache* 8): hence the well-known conclusion of the Lord's Prayer in the Textus Receptus of Matt. 6:13. What this perhaps means is that, at the beginning of the Christian era, the individualizing of seals in Jewish benedictions had not as yet proceeded very far; and it was destined to make no progress in Christianity, because of the New Testament teaching that it is through, or in the name of, Christ that prayer and thanksgiving are acceptable to God (Jn. 15:16; 16:23-27; Rom. 1:8; Eph. 5:20; Heb. 13:15 etc.). The phrase 'through Jesus Christ' already appears in one of the above seals from the *Didache*, as it does at the end of several of the benedictions of the Christianized Tephillah (*Apostolic Constitutions* 7:35, 37f.); and this phrase was to grow into the sort of standard Trinitarian doxology that concludes Hippolytus's consecration prayer.

A sixth point is that the congregational response of 'Amen' to Christian thanksgivings (1 Cor. 14:16 etc.) is the same that was used with Jewish benedictions in the synagogue, as the Tosephta records (Tos. Sukkah 4:6), and the same that is found, still earlier, in the Old Testament (1 Chr. 16:36; Neh. 8:6).

A final point is that, both in Hippolytus's doxology and in the seals of the *Didache*, the word 'glory' (Gk. *doxa*, Lat. *gloria*) is evidently used as another equivalent of the Hebrew 'blessed' (*baruk*).[71]

This essay began by stressing the difficulties of the task it was attempting, and must end by disavowing any claim of finality for its conclusions. It will be obvious that the writer had benefited from the work of many earlier labourers in the field, and it may be that he ought to have benefited more; but if, with their help, he has done anything to lighten the labours of those who come next to the task, he will have achieved his aim.

---

[71] This equation is fully illustrated in Eric Werner, 'The Doxology in Synagogue and Church', published in 1945-46 and reprinted in Petuchowski's *Contributions to the Scientific Study of Jewish Liturgy (ut supra)*.

JOINT LITURGICAL STUDIES—1987 TITLES

1. **(LS49) Daily and Weekly Worship—from Jewish to Christian** (March 1987) by R. T. Beckwith, Warden of Latimer House, Oxford

   Christianity arose in a Jewish context, and Christian worship bears marks of the fact. This becomes clearest when Jewish worship of the first century is investigated, so far as evidence allows, and is compared with primitive Christian worship. This Study concentrates on daily and weekly worship.

2. **(LS 50) The Canons of Hippolytus** (June 1987) edited by Paul Bradshaw, Professor of Liturgics, University of Notre Dame

   These Canons, only available in manuscript in Arabic, reflect a Greek original which has been variously dated by scholars, but is here located in the early fourth century. This makes it the earliest source for Hippolytus himself. The major modern edited version of the text has been of R. G. Coquin in French (1966), but a full English translation has never been published before. This makes the publication a notable contribution to our understanding of a period of liturgical history from which extant materials are scanty.

3. **(LS 51) Modern Anglican Ordination Rites** (September 1987) edited by Colin Buchanan, Bishop of Aston

   The modern liturgical texts of the Anglican Churches have been starting in recent years to include ordination rites, going beyond the '1662 Tradition' which was well documented in Paul Bradshaws's Alcuin Club book, *The Anglican Ordinal* (S.P.C.K. 1971). The revisions of the last 15 years throughout the Anglican Communion are collected and presented by Colin Buchanan, who has here done for ordination rites what he has done three times in the last decades for eucharistic rites. The collection is timed to make texts available for study prior to the Lambeth Conference.

4. **(LS 52) Models of Liturgical Theology** (December 1987) by James Empereur, of the Jesuit School of Theology, Berkeley

   Theological pluralism has significant implications for the theology of worship. It is no longer possible to speak of *the* liturgical theology. There are several approaches to theological reflection on the experience of the church's liturgy. There are many models of liturgical theology. Worship may be characterized differently, depending on the dominant model at work, such as liturgy as institution, as mystery, as sacrament, as proclamation, as process, as therapeutic, and as liberation. No one model exhausts the meaning of the liturgy; no one model can be omitted from an adequate theological understanding of the worship of the assembly.

Recent Alcuin titles (obtainable through booksellers, or via Grove Books Limited, post-free).

1980 *The Communion of Saints* (by Michael Perham) S.P.C.K. £6.95
1981 *Daily Prayer in the Early Church* (by Paul Bradshaw) S.P.C.K. £6.95
1982 *Nuptial Blessing* (by Kenneth Stevenson) S.P.C.K. £10.50
1983 *The Godly Order* (by Geoffrey Cuming) S.P.C.K. £8.50
1984 *Latest Anglican Liturgies 1976-1984* (edited by Colin Buchanan) S.P.C.K. (hardback) £25
1985 *The Meaning of Baptism* (by Raymond Burnish) S.P.C.K. £10.50
1986 *Earth and Altar* (by Donald Gray) Canterbury Press £10.50
Also 'Alcuin Club Manuals'
No. 1 *The Eucharist* (by Michael Perham) S.P.C.K. 1981, £2.25
No. 3 *Family Services* (by Kenneth Stevenson) S.P.C.K., 1981, £2.25

Grove Liturgical Studies

This series began in March 1975, and has been published quarterly. Nos. 1, 3-6 and 10 are out of print. Asterisked numbers have been reprinted. Prices in 1987, £2.

DATE DUE

MAY 27 '89		
NOV 08 1999		
OCT 3 '99		
APR 16 2001		

HIGHSMITH   #LO-45220